MW00743537

Windows
to
Albania

1998-99 NWMS READING BOOKS

RESOURCE BOOK FOR THE LEADER

IMAGINE THE HARVEST
Edited by Beverlee Borbe

FOR THE READER

AGAINST THE TIDE
The Miracle of Growth in the Netherlands
By Cisca Verwoerd

DAUGHTER OF AFRICA
The Story of Juliet Ndzimandze
By Charles Gailey

JUST CAUSE
How Nazarene Students Are Changing Their World
By Frank Moore

PLACES CALLED INDIA
By Tim Crutcher

PREACHER WITH A MISSION
The Story of Nina Griggs Gunter
By Helen Temple

WINDOWS TO ALBANIA
By Connie Griffith Patrick

Windows
to
Albania

by Connie Griffith Patrick

Nazarene Publishing House
Kansas City, Missouri

Contents

Connie Griffith Patrick and her husband, Bill, have served as Nazarenes in Volunteer Service in three assignments, including Papua New Guinea and Albania. They presently teach at European Nazarene Bible College. They graduated from Pasadena/Point Loma Nazarene College. Connie grew up as a missionary kid in New Zealand where her parents, R. E. and Dorothy Griffith, pioneered that field.

Prologue

"You can go to Albania, and you can leave tomorrow!"

My husband, Bill, and I had just finished a six-month assignment as Nazarenes in Volunteer Service (NIVS) in Papua New Guinea. We had organized and taught in the first missionary kids' school on the hospital compound at Kudjip in the Western Highlands Province. Now, we were standing by the World Mission booth at the 1993 General Assembly of the Church of the Nazarene in Indianapolis, talking with David Hayse, then head of missionary personnel. We had found David 30 seconds before, and Bill half-jokingly slapped him on the shoulder and said, "So, David, where are you going to send us next?" All I heard was, "Albania . . . tomorrow!"

I am not proud of the fact that I did not know the location of Albania. I vaguely remembered reading somewhere that Mother Teresa was from Albania, and I had stared at her picture thinking, "Hm! So that's what an Albanian looks like."

Before we could ask, "What, where, or who is Albania?" David became more serious. "We need someone in there as soon as possible to help David and Sandi Allison," he said. "I would like you to talk to a man named Hermann Gschwandtner. He has been there and knows more about it than I do. Would you be willing to meet with him? If so, I'll set up an appointment."

We nodded our heads, somewhat dazed. "Good! Check back with my secretary in a few hours, and she will give you the details of your appointment." We were feeling a combination of numbness and excitement as we walked away.

"Lord, is this why we felt so impressed to be here for General Assembly?" we asked. We had not even finished unpacking our bags from Papua New Guinea and barely had enough time to get here before Assembly started. "Lord, is this why we are here? Is this what You have in mind?"

We were to meet with Hermann Gschwandtner the next day. While we were waiting for our appointment time, I stood watching a video in the Compassionate Ministries booth. There were various scenes of children with outstretched arms being given food, and pictures of ox-drawn hay carts on dilapidated roads. But the face that burned its way into my mind and heart was a weather-beaten old woman dressed in black, from the scarf around her head to her worn skirt and socks. She, too, needed the food that was being given. But when she turned from the aid truck, the eyes that met mine through the video screen were eyes of confusion and helplessness. Underneath, I could see a warmth and a hunger for love. We stared at each other for a long moment, then the video faded and was finished.

I discovered tears running down my cheeks and felt a deep sense of compassion. "What was the matter with me?" I thought. "I must be really tired." I did not even know where this lady was from. Just then, Bill called me saying Hermann was there.

Hermann Gschwandtner was intense. He definitely had a calling and a mission—to find the right people for ministry in Eastern Europe. He did not know if we would be the ones to be a part of it, but he gave us the facts. "You can pray about it and see if God will use you in this exciting opportunity to minister to a people in a country that tried to ban God for nearly 50 years. The conditions are rough, the pressures tough, and our new missionaries have a young boy and a baby under a year old. If you believe this is what God wants, we need you there as soon as possible."

Even as he was talking I began to feel my heart grow warm, but I do not remember asking many questions. We did not know what questions to ask. We felt stunned. Our thoughts were scrambling, and no words surfaced.

Bill stood to leave. "We will certainly pray about it and let you know in a few days if we feel it is something we should pursue." We all agreed and shook hands. As we started to leave, I turned back to Rev. Gschwandtner. "By the way," I asked, "the video playing in the Compassionate Ministries booth, what country are they showing?"

"Albania," he said.

* * * * *

Almost four weeks in Albania and I have not yet written in my journal. I guess I fear that thoughts of any depth would be negative. I haven't yet written my dearest friends for the same reason. But now my niece has written asking for a view of Albania through my eyes, and I am forced to face my thoughts, to pull them out and look at them and admit what they are.

One day last week, our third week in Albania, we were driving into the countryside to the relief warehouses in order to check on some medical supplies. The green rolling hills, the budding vineyards, and even a few tall trees that somehow had escaped the axe were bringing warmth back into my soul.

The place we now call home is surrounded by five-story concrete tenement buildings devoid of any architectural beauty or color except for occasional window coverings or brightly colored pieces of laundry hanging from the tiny balconies. These tenements, called *pallati* (apartments), tower over dirty, broken streets strewn with trash and garbage and children playing the games that children play the world over. That is the way it is when I look down or across. But when I look up, I can see the top of a green, hand-terraced hill—bare except for grass, but green nevertheless. I must lift my eyes to the hills more often.

The sky is usually gray or dirty due to the spring storms and the nearby factory that belches huge amounts of black smoke into the atmosphere. But this day we were out in the countryside, and my husband of nearly 30 years could see the light coming back into my eyes. He leaned over with a soft smile and said quietly, "God has given you a great love and desire for the beautiful. Now you must ask Him to give you an acceptance of the ugly."

Tears swelled behind my eyes, then forced their way to the surface where I struggled to keep them from betraying my emotions. The truth of his statement bit deeply into my heart. I wavered between love for him and his sensitivity to who I am and what I need, and anger that I should have to accept the ugly. "O God, why and how? I cannot! Show me. Teach me. How can I accept the ugly any more than You can accept sin?" I was screaming it inside, almost defiantly. And in the painful quiet that followed my silent outburst I had my answer.

"You, Lord, look past the ugliness of our sin, without accepting it, to the beauty that You created in us to reflect yourself," I prayed. "You focus on what there is to love, not on what there is to hate. You did what You could to change the hateful, offering yourself and dying for our sins so that by believing and trusting in You, we may be made clean and restored to beauty.

"But I cannot do that, Lord, at least the dying and restoring part. However, with Your power working in me

- I can focus on what there is to love and not on what there is to hate;
- I can look past the toilet that we flush by dipping water from a trash can and beyond the window that is missing a third of its glass to the children who have no knowledge of who Jesus is, and think of ways to reach out to them;
- I can look past the rough, gray concrete floor tiles and the bed that defies description, to the satin quilt with a piece of exquisite, homemade cutwork lace tacked around the edge— a gift from our landlady, who wanted to make something beautiful for us;
- I can look past the drab, broken, garbage-strewn pallati to the people they hold inside

and lovingly, longingly pray for them to know the Author of life and beauty.

"Lord, You are so good at this kind of thing. Would You live Your life in me? Pour Your love through me. Help me to die to the unimportant in order that what is important and valid can be victorious and produce something beautiful in Your name. Thank You, Father. So be it."

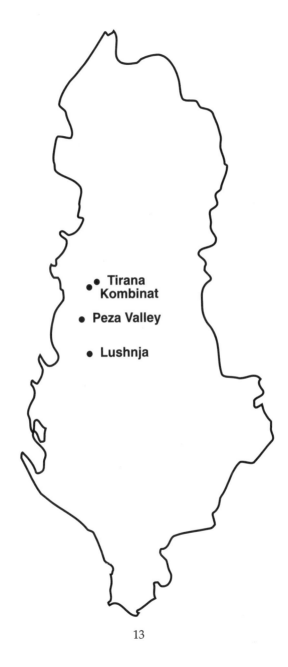

• • Tirana
Kombinat

• Peza Valley

• Lushnja

PART 1

Windows to Hearts

An English Class

EVERY DAY AS I WALKED DOWN the narrow street behind our pallat, I passed two small food stands. The first belonged to <u>Drita</u>, where I bought eggs, honey, and jam (when it was available). The second I passed without buying anything because it had so few items. But I always greeted the owners or waved and smiled.

One afternoon a young woman in her 30s, whose name I later learned was <u>Mariana</u>, was there and greeted me in English. I stopped, walked back, and asked, "Do you speak English?"

"A little," she replied.

We conversed "a little" and I left. The next time I was passing, she called to me. "Why are you here in Albania?" The tone of voice was neither antagonistic nor friendly, just curious.

I took a deep breath. God and I had been working that very morning on what I should give as an answer to this common question. "For over 23 years we have known and loved God, and for over 23 years Albania has not been allowed to know

God. We have come to tell Albanians about God and His Son, Jesus."

Mariana either didn't understand or wouldn't accept my answer. She asked again, "But why have you come?"

I hesitated, then the answer burst from somewhere within. "Because we love Jesus . . . and we love you."

She looked at me in disbelief but didn't respond. The conversation was over. I said, "Mirupafshim" (Good-bye), and continued down the street—praying like mad. "O God, You are awesome! Thank You for helping me to say that. Help it to sink deep into her heart."

A few days later, I was on my way to the health clinic to meet with several doctors and a few neighborhood people for English classes. No one showed up that day except Dr. Genci and Dr. Shpresa. We were discussing the fact that *shpresa* is the Albanian word for "hope." The English course was based on the Book of Mark. As we read the scripture for that day, Dr. Genci said, "Dr. Fabiola doesn't believe in God!" There was a hint of a challenge, wanting my reaction.

"I know," I said, "and that is so sad." They were quiet, waiting as I continued, "Because without God there is no hope!"

As they processed those English words into their own language and the realization of what I had said broke through to their understanding, their faces brightened. They smiled and shook their heads, which in Albania means "yes" or "we understand." From that day on there was an openness and a willingness of spirit as we read and discussed the actions and claims of the living Christ.

All the way home I was saying, "Yes, God! You are awesome! You gave me those words! You provided that opportunity. Working for You is fantastic. I love it!"

A few days later, on class day, Mariana (the lady in the second food stand) stopped me to ask where I was going. I told her I was teaching an English class.

"Can I be in the class?" she asked.

"Well, the class is full right now. But if there is an opening, I will tell you."

By the next week everyone in the class had dropped out except for Dr. Genci and Dr. "Hope," so Mariana was invited. The second time she came, we closed the class with Jesus' statement, "Come unto me all you who are tired and carrying heavy burdens and I will give you rest." We discussed the meaning of each word as we translated it. I could tell they were thinking hard. As they left the room, Mariana blurted out, "But it's so hard to believe in Jesus when we've been taught for 23 years there is no God."

"I know," I told her. "But God will help you because He is real! Ask Him and He *will* help you. I, too, will pray that you can believe."

One day as we were learning the Lord's Prayer, Mariana exclaimed excitedly, "I have heard this! I know about this! My grandmother taught us this when I was a little girl!"

Again God had been faithful. He had left His witness with a grandmother to pass on to her little grandchildren, whispering to them in the dark of the night, "Do not say this to anyone, but God *is* real!"

Mariana's brother, Romeo, says that because of his grandmother's teaching, he always believed, in spite of the educational brainwashing of the Communist regime. But Mariana, an engineer of high standing in the textile factory of Kombinat, had believed the lies and even made fun of others who, after the fall of Communism, professed to believe. Now, however, things are different. She is telling her workmates, "I do believe in Jesus. He *is* real."

English class from Book of Mark. To Connie's right, Dr. Genci and her left, Mariana. Dr. Shpresa on far right of the picture.

It's Too Late for Me!

One of Bill's assignments was to have 10 hymns translated from the Nazarene hymnal. Through the help of another missionary, he was introduced to Alqi Kristo. Alqi was a 70-year-old poet who had translated works of Shakespeare into Albanian.

The criteria for the translation of hymns was fourfold:

- The meaning must be the same.
- The lines must rhyme.
- There must be the same number of syllables in each line as in English.
- The stress of the words must fall on the correct beat of the music.

This was a difficult order, but Alqi accomplished it beautifully.

We had been praying that the words of these hymns would speak to Alqi and bring the light of Jesus to his darkness. During one of their editing sessions, he and Bill began to talk about the meaning of the words, and Alqi expressed admiration for their beauty.

"Alqi, is this something you desire for your life?"

"I'm too old. It's too late for me."

We tried to dissuade him, but he shook his head sadly. It broke our hearts to feel the hopelessness of his response.

Later I wrote home: "On the surface there is the characteristic warm Albanian hospitality, but beneath that warmth there is almost a heart deafness. It is as if their hearts and minds have been so seared and scarred with the lies of atheism that now, even though the old regime is gone, the fear of not being able to provide for their families together with the hopelessness of unbelief has left a seemingly impenetrable void. But thank God, He is in the business of 'opening blind eyes, unstopping deaf ears and bringing to life those that are dead' [see Matt. 11:5]. Although these words were written centuries ago, they are a vivid description of what we sense here."

The One Who Cried

I had just received word that Besim died. The Lord is my shepherd, but He was not the shepherd of Besim's family.

"O God, what more could I have done or said to lead <u>Besim</u> to You?" I prayed. "I avoided him as much as I could because he was almost always so very drunk. What can we do now with <u>Yrena</u> and her mom to let them discover You?"

My mind went back to the day I was baby-sitting at the Allisons' home, sitting on the second-story balcony and writing while the baby slept. A car pulled up in front of the house next door, a red Mercedes. I didn't pay any attention until I heard voices get louder, followed by pleading.

Yrena and her mother were trying to get Besim out of the car. He was drunk again. Many times he had staggered toward our vehicle as we were driving down the road. David always stopped and, shaking his hand through the van window, asked how he was. The answer was always so slurred it was unintelligible, and the saliva drizzled from his loose lips. Twice in two months I had seen him lying halfway in the road passed out.

Once as I was visiting Yrena, I saw him coming up the road to home, and I practically ran to get away before he reached the house. Yrena felt so hurt. She kept saying, "Connie, don't be afraid. Don't be afraid. He is kind. He won't hurt you." But I ran anyway.

My thoughts weave back and forth, much as Besim and his family did that day as they fought to get him from the red Mercedes into the house. In a few minutes his son emerged. I had heard he was a government official and many people paid him bribes in Raki, an Albanian whiskey. That was how Besim could afford to be drunk much of the time.

The Mercedes bumped down the rock and dirt road, spitting debris as it went. A Mercedes was strong enough to handle this rough road. But Yrena and her thin-bodied, gaunt-faced mother were not. And neither was I.

It was the day of Besim's funeral, or rather the process that takes place when someone has died. I knew I must go and that I would go alone. I was ushered into the room designated for the women. It was lined with chairs. Every available space was filled, and the women sat quietly weeping. Besim's unembalmed body was lying in the middle of the room on a bed, covered by a sheet. In spite of my remonstrances, a woman stood up and gave me her chair. It is the Albanian way. They always honor the *huaj* (foreigner). Accepting their graciousness, I sat, bowed my head respectfully toward Besim's body, and began to pray silently.

"O God, what am I doing here? I don't know the language. I don't know their customs or death rituals. Help me not to do anything dumb—anything that would make You look bad."

Besim's wife was bending over the lifeless form crying, not too loudly, but fervently declaring her love, faithfulness, and adoration for her good husband. He had dried out just two months before at a hospital facility and came home to finish building the new house he had been working on for a year. It

20

was the house we were sitting in. When he wasn't drinking, Besim was quiet, gentle, and hardworking—the exact opposite of his drunken personality.

As Besim's widow finished her mourning, Yrena, my teenage friend, moved in to take her place. She was the youngest of four children. She threw herself over the edge of the bed and poured out her grief, deep and unrestrained. She told him how much she loved him even though he drank. He was, after all, her dad. On and on, her broken heart was exposed. I was praying, "O God, somehow comfort them. Show them how much You care, even though they don't know You."

Suddenly I was the same age as Yrena, and I had thrown myself on my bed screaming out my unbelief that my dad was gone, never again able to give me a bear hug. Even though it happened 32 years before, I felt the pain as though it were yesterday—the awful sense of loss and loneliness, the physical ache in the heart. I cried for Yrena, for her mom and sisters, and for all they were feeling. Oh, how I hurt with her. And then Yrena's sister joined her, alternately screaming, crying, and wailing in unbelief, anger, and sorrow at the finality of death.

I cried with them. I couldn't stop. I realized that the women were staring at me now. I didn't care. I just knew how much I hurt for them, and how I wished I could spare them from the pain not only now but also in the days, months, and years ahead. Yrena's mother was only 41, but she will wear black the rest of her life. It is an Albanian tradition to show faithfulness to a husband's memory.

I hadn't brought a handkerchief of any kind. I didn't have anywhere to wipe the wetness that kept flowing unchecked. Finally, after kissing Yrena's sister-in-law once on each cheek, I excused myself. I walked past the bedroom where the men sat in chairs lining the walls. They talked quietly and smoked incessantly. I made my way to the porch, I put my shoes back on, and after being thanked by the politician son who was smoking outside, I left. I just wanted to get back to my tiny, cold concrete apartment where I could be alone with my grief for them and for myself. I felt I was doing so little.

"O God, what else can I do? Loving them, caring for them is not enough. I need to tell them about You . . . how wonderful You are; that You are the God of all comfort; that You cry when we cry and laugh with us in our joys; that You died to save us from the power and penalty of sin; that You are our only way out of the mess we have made of this world, our only hope; . . . but I don't speak the language."

Many days passed. When I would pass the village houses, I would overhear the ladies say softly to each other as they washed their clothes on their porches, "There goes the one who cried."

"O Jesus, thank You. Thank You for helping me to communicate. You spoke *Your* language of identification, of brokenness. You are the God who cries with us."

The Terrible Sinner

Campus Crusade for Christ had taken the *Jesus* film into the mountain areas of Albania by helicopter.

Otherwise, the only way to get to these backcountry villages was to take a bus as far as you could, then travel the remainder of the journey by foot. With the amount of equipment needed, the limits of time, and the short-term summer teams making hundreds of presentations, the helicopter was a necessity.

After the presentations, where nearly everyone in the crowd would raise a hand to show a desire to receive Christ, the teams took the names of the people and starred the names of those that were the most interested. The lists were then given to the various Evangelical mission organizations working in the country for follow-up.

One of the villages given our Nazarene missionary David Allison was Greq; a village up in the hills at the far end of the Peza Valley. He arranged for Bill and a young translator to go there and talk to the converts about holding Bible studies in their village. Since we did not have a helicopter, they drove to the end of the road, left the vehicle with a guard at the last village, and walked the remaining hour and a half to Greq.

Their list of names had one name starred— Ramiz. As they met people on the road, they asked if anyone knew a man named Ramiz.

"Oh, yes. He lives up there. He is a schoolteacher."

They kept climbing until they found his home. He greeted them with the usual Albanian hospitality and invited them in to talk over coffee.

"Are you still interested in studying the Bible?" they asked.

"Yes," he replied. "But it is so far for you to walk, and with winter coming the road will be even more difficult. I teach school in the last village, where the road ends. Every day I walk there to teach. Could I meet you there one day a week after school and study with you?"

"Yes," they replied enthusiastically. "That would be wonderful!"

The day they had set finally came. Ramiz, Bill, and the translator went to each house asking if the occupants were interested in studying the Bible. Eventually, a relative said they could study in the sitting room of his house, so they began.

Their first time together they were studying the subject of sin. Ramiz said, with despair in his voice and eyes, "For 17 years I have told the children there is no God. I am a terrible sinner." You could almost see the awful weight of guilt on his shoulders. Bill tried to explain that because of Jesus, God forgives our sins, no matter how terrible, and forgets them. But Bill sensed Ramiz was not yet able to grasp this truth.

In the Balkan cultures one neither forgives nor forgets. Consequently, it is very difficult to believe that God will forgive and forget. By the same reasoning it is hard to get across that because we are forgiven, we also must forgive and be forgiven by others.

Pray that the Albanians will understand that even though this is their culture—their old citizenship—God is extending to them a new culture, a new citizenship, where "old things have passed away; . . . [and] all things have become new" (2 Cor. 5:17).

From Silence to Singing

A *pallat* is a five-story, concrete, rectangular tenement building with no personality and little color but beige. Each pallat has three stairwells, of which each of the five floors has three two-bedroom, one-toilet apartments. Thus every stairwell leads to the homes of 15 different families. On every floor live 7 to 15 people, many encompassing three generations. This was our mission field.

In Kombinat, the suburb of Tirana where we lived, are 50-70 of these *pallati. Pallat* is the Albanian word equivalent to the English word "palace." The Communists told the Albanians they were the richest people on earth. Because they were cut off from the outside world and had no frame of reference for comparison, they believed the regime or pretended to believe for safety's sake.

Working at my tiny wooden sink one day, I heard the sound of breaking glass and ran to our third-story window to see a couple of three- or four-year-olds below smashing empty bottles on the pieces of road surface that were still intact.

I watched in horror, expecting at any time to see them cut themselves and the blood flow. However, after a few minutes they turned unharmed to the next most popular pastime, sorting through the garbage and trash dumped in a pile a few yards from our stairwell entrance.

Before the children finished, a local shepherd entered my scene, herding his small flock of sheep into the garbage area to forage for food. Then, three or four cows came with a village woman. Later, even a herd of chickens came. I say "herd" because they were literally being herded by the long stick of an old widow woman dressed in black.

The children tried to find a space between the broken glass, animal dung, and furrows of dried mud to play jump rope. Every day I heard them and saw them laughing, shouting, singing, and playing as I tried to study language, wash my clothes by hand, and walk to the open market for fresh vegetables.

"Lord," I prayed, "You must help me! I'm not a children's worker by any stretch of the imagination, but I cannot let these precious ones live and grow up within a few feet of me without knowing You. What can I do? How can I do it?" Gently He showed me His plan.

Our landlady's 15-year-old niece spoke excellent English and said she would translate for me. I had bought some child evangelism materials before we left, just in case "someone else" might use them. I told only the school-age children on our stairwell that I was going to have a Good News Club.

There was just one problem. In my living/kitchen and eating area there was room for only 10 children, so 5 of them could invite one friend. Every Thursday for months, I had between 10 and 15 children on the chairs and on the floor learning the glorious truths about Jesus.

"He is your Friend who is preparing a beautiful home for you in heaven, where there will be no more sickness, poverty, cold, or death," I would say. You should have seen their eyes get wide and their faces shine with hope when we read together the biblical description of heaven. Three to four years ago, they had never heard the name of Jesus and wouldn't have dared to whisper it if they had, let alone sing it at the tops of their lungs as they did in our _pallat._

I found myself praying, "O God, what joy! What an incredible privilege! Nothing this world has to offer even comes close to this kind of excitement—to the exploding fulfillment of carrying out Your Great Commission to 'go and tell'!"

Good News club in our apartment

When I opened the door at three o'clock every Thursday, they were pushing so hard and were so excited to be there they practically fell into my hall. The second they were inside, they hurriedly took off their shoes and ran to get one of the few seats (Albanians often remove their shoes when they enter a home). None of us had vacuum cleaners, so it really helped to leave as much dirt and germs as possible at the door.

27

We learned action songs and drew colored pictures to illustrate biblical truths. They were very careful with the crayons I gave them to use and treated them like gold. I noticed they seemed to always be in a hurry, as if someone were going to snatch the precious crayons away before they were finished.

They all learned to pray, and some prayed like bishops. They memorized verse after verse of Scripture with ease. When they could say it perfectly, I gave them stars for each verse, and they placed them on a chart. Someone from the United States donated a whole packet of shiny red, silver, and blue stars. The day we chose red stars there was an uncomfortable gasp from a couple of older girls, followed by embarrassed giggles. In answer to my questioning look, they explained, "Red stars are for Communism." We quickly got rid of the red stars.

They listened carefully each week as we laid the foundation of the story of God. When I sensed they were ready, I asked if they wanted to ask Jesus to enter their heart and life and be their Lord and Savior. All responded with a fervent yes! We will not know the depth of these commitments until we reach heaven.

When the time came to leave, I prayed silently as I helped each one with his or her coat. "O God, keep them in Your Word. Protect them. They are Your lambs."

I watched from my window as they reached the ground floor and tried to find a somewhat clear surface to play a crude game of hopscotch. The shepherd was there again looking for food for his sheep.

Is there a thread that ties all of this together? The scene was a garbage dump of hopelessness, corruption, and brokenness. Enter the Shepherd who gave His life for the sheep, and the Lamb who was slain before the foundation of the world so that children and everyone else—whoever will listen—can sing a new song.

This song was written by Arjan, an Albanian teenage believer:

Oh, you who are tired, where are you going?
Come, the Lord is inviting you.
Wake up sons. Oh, wake up all.
The Lord is standing close.
Open your heart to Him.
Oh, if life is difficult and you want to find peace,
Today if you want — receive.
Tomorrow may be too late.

PART 2

Windows to History

Ancient Windows

I WALKED THE STREETS OF TIRANA, watching the kaleidoscope of faces. "Who are these people?" I thought. "From where have they come? What has made them the way they are?" The expressions were often purposely blank, but some couldn't disguise their curiosity as they looked at me, an American. "What are they thinking?" I wondered.

I was told the answers to all my questions lie in history. So I searched in various places to ferret out some answers, to somehow understand and hopefully share my understanding with others.

Albanians are the descendants of the Thraco-Illyrians, who were about the oldest race in Europe, and a distinctive and fiercely independent people. This is illustrated by their own name for their country—*Shqiperia* (shcheep-uh-REE-ah), which means "eagle's country."

Annexed by Rome in 168 B.C., Albania, then called Illyricum, was visited by the apostle Paul. There is some evidence that Titus was martyred in

30

Durres in the Roman amphitheater, so we know that Christianity had early roots in this land.

After Rome's fall, it is a wretchedly repetitive story as Albania was invaded time after time and driven down the road to impoverishment until they were the most backward country in Europe. The interesting thing is that the Albanians went right on fighting and resisting the whole time.

In 1468, Albania fell to the Ottoman Empire, so anyone who considered life more important than allegiance to Christ became a Muslim. The Turks ruled Albania for 450 years, during which time the country remained undeveloped and neglected. Although as a people they were still not absorbed, their culture was greatly impacted by the Turkish-Muslim influence. As late as 1945, 70 percent of the people registered Islam as their religion.

Through the battering of two world wars, the Albanians never gave up the struggle for freedom, finally attaining it after Hitler's troops were ousted in 1944. Now, however, the greatest enemy of freedom was internal and proved to be the most formidable of all. So began what some have titled the Years of Terror.

Were Any Faithful?

The Communist Party was founded in 1941 and was strongly molded by Enver Hoxha, the emerging leader. Those who were against having a Communist regime were the first to feel the heavy blows of this rigid, Stalinist-style dictator. Catholics had actually begun to experience persecution as early as 1944. The excuse was that since Catholicism was centered in Italy and Austria, and both Mussolini's and Hitler's forces had occupied Albania, they wanted nothing left of Italian or Austrian influences. By 1982, 200 priests and leaders had been executed or died in horrendous labor camps and prisons.

Soon, however, it became clear that the Communist leaders were taking a very hard stance against all religious practice. By the time Hoxha died (1985), there was little of any religion remaining and certainly none known to the authorities. Every speck of faithfulness that was discovered was eradicated from society with the intent of "purging with finality the 'opiate of the people.'"

These terror-filled years could also be called "the reign of secrecy." With very few exceptions, no one on the inside of Albania knew what was happening in the outside world, and no one on the outside knew what was happening in Albania. Enver Hoxha played on the lessons of history to promote fear of other countries, but in reality other countries no longer cared about Albania. With his magnetic personality, Hoxha persuaded his people to believe they had the highest standard of living in the world and that they must protect themselves from the many enemies preparing to take what they had. This was the reason given for the people being virtually imprisoned within their own borders.

Even the children were taught to recognize a foreigner, and spearheads were placed on every field post to impale the paratroopers when they came. Hoxha built approximately 800,000 concrete military bunkers, which blight the entire country-side of Albania. It is said that there is enough concrete in these bunkers to build a house for every family in Albania. He had managed to pull off one of the 20th century's greatest con jobs.

Anyone disagreeing with Hoxha's policies in any area to any degree, no matter what their position in society, was not tolerated. These persons were declared "enemies of the people," and for this crime the punishment was at least removal from job and home and, at most, liquidation or internment in the cruel labor camps. Death was preferred to internment, and some found ways to commit suicide rather than live another day in such incredibly tortuous conditions. Hundreds more, their bodies and minds unable to withstand the demonic treatment, died while imprisoned.

A high percentage of the population was coerced into or paid for spying on their own families and neighbors. The result was that no one could trust anyone else. The people that spied, many times giving false testimony in order to receive payment, were called 10-lek people. For 10 lek (Albanian pennies), they would turn in their neighbors to the *sigurimi* (secret police).

Along with many other provisions, Albanians were limited to only one government-controlled television channel. If the sigurimi saw a television antenna facing toward Italy, they would question or blacklist the violator.

The savagery of the repression of all real and imagined opposition to the dictator Hoxha was such that 700,000 Albanians were killed outright or imprisoned for long periods in prisons or labor camps. At one such place, the prisoners' job was to drain swamplands with a few basic implements and their bare hands. Many times, whole families were sent to the labor camps. The party gained support for the persecution of church leaders by saying that imprisoned minds and the low estate of women were the result of religion and the church.

Our friend, Thoma Qiriazi, tells of his experience during these years. "Being now age 56, I have lived through the entire 45-year period of the Communist regime in Albania. These years can be divided into two periods. From 1945 to 1967 religious faith was still allowed, though some were persecuted harshly. My parents were Christians, and when I was small, my father often told me stories from the life of Jesus. I learned well that Jesus was our Lord and to Him we should pray and seek forgiveness. I went to church with my parents and friends. In the evenings, I prayed the Lord's Prayer. I learned only after 1990 that this prayer was the model that Jesus taught His disciples.

"During that time the atheistic propaganda of the Communist state of Albania was very strong. Almost every lesson in school spoke against religion, trying, often successfully, to argue that religion is merely a dogma, that there is no God, that Jesus Christ never existed, and so on. There were no books about God written or published in our country, and none were allowed to be imported. Under these conditions, without any direct contact with the Bible and with the pressure of this propaganda, my faith in Jesus began to waver. I began to question the existence of God and ceased to pray. Deep in my conscience, however, not every vestige of faith had disappeared. Under pressure, my mind would go again to God, but only in difficult situations."

By 1967, Hoxha was becoming desperate. An atheistic education and brutality toward people with faith in God was not bringing about the desired result. Hoxha called on the "sharp knife of the Party" to be used in the people's struggle against religious ideology. "Religion is the opiate of the people," he said, "and we must do our utmost to ensure that this trust is understood by everyone, even those who are poisoned by it. We shall have to cure them. All of our patriotic and revolutionary spirit will be required for the fight."

In a matter of weeks Hoxha dared to do something no one else had dared to do (at least in this century). He declared the abolition of all religion, and Albania became the first self-proclaimed atheist state in the world. Even Hitler and Stalin were not guilty of this. Later, Hoxha claimed it as one of his greatest achievements.

Thoma continues, "The war of the classes was extended to the war against faith, and the spreading of religious ideas became punishable by law. In the schools and textbooks antireligious propaganda was intensified even more than before. Under these conditions a return to faith could not even be discussed. While working as a teacher, high school principal, and university professor, I told my students there was no scientific basis for religious faith in general and Christianity in particular."

Teams of party youth under the auspices of the government were dispatched throughout the country to "convince" people to give up their religious beliefs and to destroy places of worship. The purge, which was designed to suppress every trace of religion, lasted a year and a half. Twenty-one hundred churches, convents, mosques, and other religious institutions were burned or utterly destroyed. Only a small number of edifices of artistic, cultural, or historic value were spared, and these were secularized.

All crosses, even those on tombstones, were removed so that no memory of Christ would remain. One source stated that on every tombstone in the land, the Cross was replaced with a red star, the symbol of the Communist atheistic state.

Dates in Albania were referred to as the "second century before our era" or the "fourth century of our era" instead of B.C. or A.D. In the English-Albanian dictionary, these definitions are given:

- God—The world was not created by god but by evolution of matter in the universe.
- Faith—Have faith in people, in our own efforts, in friendship.

Sometime after the purge, our friend Ylli was on a championship indoor futbol (soccer) team. He was afforded the honor of playing in the final game. It was to be held in one of the cathedrals that had been turned into a sports center. There was little left that would cause one to guess that at one time this was a church. Even so, he felt his heart pulling him to think about what this building had been like when God was worshiped there.

Ylli's grandmother had told him about God when he was a little boy. Somehow that truth had gripped his heart, and in all the years of growing up with militant atheistic teaching, he had never given up his faith that God is real, that we can worship Him and know Him, and that He helps us. Slowly, he walked around the interior, touched the walls, and tried to imagine what it would be like to worship God again openly. He thought he was alone, but suddenly someone yelled at him angrily, "What do you think you are doing? Get away from there!" Ylli quickly complied and disappeared.

Ylli knew the results of any hint of religious activity. Suspicion would cause questioning and subsequent punishment. If a young man was 15 or under, he might not be sent to the internment camps, but his name would be put on a blacklist that would prevent him from ever being hired for a job or getting an education. He would become a burden to his family, and no one in their right mind would ever allow their daughter to marry him. He would be an outcast, walking free, but still imprisoned.

Even the threat of all of that could not keep Ylli from wondering about God. Fourteen years later, we sat in Ylli's home opening the Scriptures for him and his family—reading, explaining, and praying together. What a joy! What a privilege to be people that the Book of Romans refers to as having "beautiful feet" (see Rom. 10:15).

In spite of the cruel and inhumane measures of 1967-68, religion still survived. In a 1973 publication of the *Bashkimi* the party stated that "we have by no means achieved complete emancipation from the remnants of religious influences." They were correct in this assessment. If they had known of the grandmothers who, while rocking their grandchildren to sleep, spoke very quietly of a God who created, loved, and died for them, they would have snuffed out their lives. But they did not know, for hearts and minds are secret places where governments cannot tread. And even though the threat was "to wipe the faithful off the face of the earth," they were unable to accomplish their mission.

Some children did as they were taught in the labour youth organizations and exposed the faith of their parents and grandparents, but some treasured these things in their hearts. Still others, rejecting these truths at the time, found it easier to believe later because Grandma had tilled the soil when they were young and tender.

Violeta was a young mother in 1952. The fact of religious persecution was already a grim reality, but she would not be stopped. When she felt it was time for her children to be baptized, she very carefully made plans and carried them out. Pulling the curtains and closing the shutters, she ceremoniously provided the sacrament of baptism for her children in the family bathtub. Talk about the priesthood of believers! Violeta was a believer and her children's priest. She would do everything in her power to bring them to God.

If the sigurimi had known the truth about a little lady in the southeastern town of Korcha, we probably would not know the rest of the story. She would be just another statistic of those who were killed or died under the savage treatment in the work camps.

But she had managed to carefully hide under her Spartan bed a box that held for her a sacrificial treasure. When the first Evangelical missionaries came in 1991, she crawled under the bed and with tears of joy pulled out the box and presented it to them. Inside was a collection of money. It was not a great amount to be sure, because she had so very little. What is remarkable is that she had been faithfully collecting and saving it for 47 years. It was her tithe! A love gift to God and His kingdom. She had never given up her faith or hope, and she wanted to be found obedient.

Broken Windows

In 1985, the most powerful man in the history of Albania, the one who had set himself and his entire political machine against God, died. However, a writer who visited four years later said that within a few minutes of leaving one's hotel room, it was easy to realize that Hoxha was still ruling from the grave. But by 1992, a Tirana teacher talked freely about the effects of Hoxha's doctrine on her formative years.

"His teachings became part and parcel of our daily lives. We had to carry them out without argument. That's why Albanians became like robots. We all thought the same way, behaved the same way, dressed the same way, and lived our lives the same way because we had only his teachings to guide us. They were our 'holy bible,' sacred in every way, and it seemed life made no sense without them.

"When Hoxha died, people cried by the thousands. If you dared to come out onto the streets with lipstick on, even if you were a young bride, you would have risked being severely criticized for not mourning such a hero. Everyone was devastated. Because he had indoctrinated people with his frenzied ideology, they thought everything was lost."

In May 1990, the anticommunist movement that had swept across Eastern Europe was heading toward Albania. Our friend Thoma comments, "In 1991 I worked in an important position in the national government administration for the educational and cultural sector. The democratic process had not yet begun, and the Communist Party continued in power. However, there was a softening of the war of the classes due to the economic crises affecting Eastern Europe, including Albania. The Communist reign was gradually becoming weaker."

Thousands of Albanians fled the country. Some walked across rugged mountains to Greece and Yugoslavia. Others crossed the Adriatic in boats to seek asylum in Italy. But they were refused entry and by the thousands were forcibly returned.

At home they found their land gripped by lawlessness and unrest. For several weeks the situation was almost total anarchy. You can understand this better when you grasp the picture of a people physically and mentally imprisoned in this tiny country, almost suffocated by the most repressive, rigid form of Communism. The ordinary person had no access to the outside world. Fear and poverty ruled their lives. Individual creativity had been so stifled that the incentive to work hard and produce something of quality was crushed.

40

The blind loyalty to the man who had exercised control over their minds for so long now turned to revulsion, hate, and an intent to destroy everything that reminded them of their slavery and deception. The youth were the most radical, and with one half of the population being under 30 years of age, there were plenty of eager hands. The bronze and stone statues of Enver Hoxha, which used to tower over the center of many towns, were torn down and broken to pieces. There was hardly a window left unbroken in any school, factory, or collective-farm greenhouse in the entire land.

Then came a period of utter shock and phlegmatic despair. They had been isolated before due to the restrictions of the government. Now they were isolated because no one wanted them.

In 1992 the Democratic Party came into power, but by then the country was in economic chaos. The people were in line for hours just to get bread. There was no fuel, and firewood was quickly running out. Today, along many roads and on many hills, there is hardly a tree left standing, such was the desperation for warmth. The shops were empty—no meat, no fish, and no coffee. Seventy to 80 percent of the adult population were out of work. They had been dictated to for so long that they could not think for themselves. No one went to the fields. They sat in their homes in despair.

It was to this Albania that the Church of the Nazarene came.

PART 3

Windows to the Church

The Window Opens— the Church Enters

AT FIRST THE CHURCH OF THE NAZARENE "visited" Albania in the person of Rev. Hermann Gschwandtner. He did not know a soul in Albania but had carried a burden on his heart for Eastern Europe for many years. He arrived in Tirana, the capital, for the first time in February 1992.

Albania was one of the last of the European Communist countries to admit that Communism had failed. They changed their legal position on religion from being the most closed in the world to being the most open. The new government hoped that religion could help stem the tide of crime that was sweeping the country. Rev. Gschwandtner was there just seven months after the door opened.

Imagine how he must have felt the first time he set foot in Albania. As he walked from the plane to the customs building, he could not help but notice the weeds growing through the broken concrete path. The building gave the appearance of a residence where people had either been absent a long time or did not care. It looked temporary and unkempt.

What was he thinking as he worked his way between the staring people to the outside door? Foreigners were still a rare sight in 1992. Surely he thought about the fact that two and a half years earlier, the sigurimi was still intact and in force. He must have known that only a few months before, the majority of the Albanian people had stayed locked in their houses, afraid to even buy food because of the angry mobs destroying things and people linked to their past. Not only was the activity aimed at those they blamed, but it was also a massive rebellion against all law and order, an unrestrained expression of their freedom. They were free to rape, rob, loot, or do whatever else they felt like doing, with no fear of God or man. "Everyone did what was right in his own eyes" (Judg. 17:6).

Hermann had the name of one person to contact in Albania. Gesina Blaauw, a little lady from the Netherlands, was the head of an organization called God Loves Albania. She was among the first to come to Albania, but the only one, at that time, who stayed. Her name was given to Rev. Gschwandtner when doing his homework—meeting with people from all walks of life who have any knowledge about the place in which he is interested.

Surely Hermann was praying for protection, direction, and wisdom as he chose transportation to Tirana and found his way to Gesina. As he saw the effects of the too-recent violent attacks all around him, he could have asked himself, "Why? And what am I doing here?"

Who is Rev. Hermann Gschwandtner and why was he there? Dr. Franklin Cook, the regional director of the Eurasia Region, describes him accurately as an amazing, energized visionary who knows no boundaries. This minister of the Good News has been directly involved with six of the entries the Church of the Nazarene has made into the former Communist countries of Eastern Europe. His passion was to share the story of Jesus with the peoples of Eastern Europe, who have so long been denied exposure to the truth. When he started working in these countries, he had no personnel. The Soviet Union was ruled by the Communists, with no sign of them losing power or the country breaking apart. This was nine years before taking his present assignment as coordinator of Nazarene Compassionate Ministries International, Eurasia Region, giving him a total of 15 years work in Eastern Europe.

February is cold in Albania with wet winds that chill to the bone. Perhaps the low temperature was felt in Rev. Gschwandtner's spirit as he saw the fear and despair of the Albanians surrounding him. For four days he listened and observed. He listened to people from all walks of life, took note of the most pressing physical, social, and educational needs, and began to think about the best ways of meeting those needs in this particular culture.

In many of these newly freed countries the government leadership is still in the hands of the same people as before the fall of Communism. They have only changed the name of their political system. Consequently, they are not very excited about bringing in organizations for the purpose of planting churches. However, with the pressure of their people and other European countries to upgrade the state of their floundering economy, they are willing to allow those organizations to enter that will do something concrete to help their situation.

The function of Compassionate Ministries in the Church of the Nazarene is to provide help for the whole person. It may be seed for the farmers to sow, tools to cultivate their gardens, water projects, sanitation units, or medical supplies. The list is almost endless. The major reason we have been allowed into many closed countries is that we have seen the need in that country and tried to meet it. As we help them to help themselves, we tell them of Jesus, the Friend who changes hearts and lives. Thoma's testimony is proof that this is the greatest help we can give them.

"In the first months of 1991, a group of foreign missionaries requested a meeting with a high-ranking government official. I was asked to meet with them along with a coworker. They expressed their desire to help the Albanian people by bringing material relief. They also said they wanted to preach among the people the good news about Jesus.

"As a sign of friendship they gave me two books of the New Testament published in the Albanian language. For the first time in my life I had a book like this in my hands. When I was small, I had heard the priest read from this book in church, but I had never held one in my hands. When they told me they would speak about God to the people and wanted my help, I was horrified. But this feeling of fear did not last long. With the New Testament in my hand, I was caught up by a great desire to read it. My hesitation and fear of persecution left me, and I promised them I would help.

"I read the New Testament with great interest. It seemed as if I was finding God again. The life of Jesus was truly fascinating, a shocking and attractive revelation to me. Through His extraordinary acts, His wonderful preaching, and His supreme sacrifice, Jesus made me His own by opening the way for me to be reconciled to God.

"Many of the messages of the New Testament left a deep imprint on my conscience. The great love of God for people is a love that does not know the limit of sacrifice, a love that defeats hatred, pride, the bad in the spirit of man, even death, and brings tolerance, forgiveness, and peace. It could not help but make a deep impression on me. Jesus taught us to have love toward all people, even toward our enemies. He acted this way in love saying, 'Father, forgive them, for they do not know what they do' (Luke 23:34).

"It was this message that our tired hearts and minds needed to hear. Jesus often said to His disciples that God is our Father. When I read this, I thought about the protection, warmth, and softness that were diametrically opposed to the morals of the time in which we were living.

"God's great desire to have a healthy and intimate relationship with us could not help but touch me. But in the Bible it is emphasized that this cannot happen without our hearts being changed. The vestiges of faith that remained deep in my conscience began to come to life. I looked at my past and saw that my relationship with God was ruined and that I needed to begin again. God, full of love, was ready to forgive me at any moment, and I was ready to accept Jesus as the Savior of my life. He was standing at my door and knocking, and I heard His voice. I prayed to God and felt not only joy but spiritual peace. Now I was not alone. I had the Almighty God at my side, who would help me and be my Counselor. The future did not frighten me any longer. My life was filled with courage and hope."

Hermann returned to Germany but before long was back in Albania, this time with Franklin Cook, Merritt Mann, Gary Morsch (a physician from Olathe, Kansas, and founder of the organization Heart to Heart), and businessman Bob Helstrom of the Helstrom Foundation. They looked at hospitals, factories, businesses, and schools. The only factory in operation was the bread factory. Dr. Morsch observed that the hospitals were in worse condition than any he had seen in the world except Cambodia.

Dr. Cook remembers, "There were restaurants open but no food to be bought. Gesina somehow found some food rations that had been designated for the forces in the Gulf War, and we were able to eat. We stayed in the largest hotel in the country. The conditions were terrible."

The main objective of this group was to register the Church of the Nazarene in Albania. The newly elected democratic officials had not developed procedures for registrations or legalizing documents. Rev. Gschwandtner was taken into one room to sign a sheaf of papers, and Dr. Cook into another. The registration was a twofold document somewhat like a dual partnership between Compassionate Ministries and the church. When they emerged from their respective rooms, they asked one of Gesina's friends, "How do you register an organization in this country when the officials are all entirely new?"

"I do not know," he responded, "but we will go to the courthouse and see what we can discover."

Dr. Cook reports, "When we arrived at the courthouse, everything was in a state of chaos. People were sitting all around on the floor. Gesina's friend found a secretary and told her something in Albanian, and she walked away with the papers. Gesina's friend explained that she was taking them to a judge for the papers to be signed. Within a few minutes she returned, signed papers in hand. As they went out the door of the courthouse, they paid the 50-lek (50-cent) fee for legal service to the cashier.

As they left the courthouse, they could hardly believe they held in their hands the legal permission to begin ministry in Albania. In light of history it was a miracle. They left the next day thanking God for His hand of love and care, which had made it possible to receive the coveted registration. The Church of the Nazarene was one of the first five organizations registered in the country of Albania.

Every month for 10 months Rev. Hermann went to Albania not only to supervise the distribution of aid but also to find adequate and safe housing for the Nazarene missionaries he believed would be coming. On one of these visits he had left a copy of the official documents of Compassionate Ministries with Thoma

Qiriazi, who by now was chairman of the Board of Advisors to the Prime Minister, and the person in charge of humanitarian-aid shipments. After studying it thoroughly, Thoma spoke to Hermann.

"Mr. Hermann, your church may be the answer for our country. We have desperate problems, but the vision of Nazarene Compassionate Ministries is just what we need. I am willing to leave my job and help you as much as I can."

"All right," Hermann answered. "I need you to accomplish these specific tasks. Here is money with which to carry them out. I will need a complete record of receipts for expenditures when I return next month."

Although Thoma had agreed, Hermann wondered if he would recoup even half of the receipts. But God had sent us a beautifully honest person in Thoma. When Hermann returned the next month, Thoma handed him receipts that accounted for every expenditure down to the last penny.

Due to the particular needs of Albania it was the recommendation of the Regional Office to the Department of World Mission that work in Albania begin with an agricultural missionary. When they checked the files, they found that God had prepared a person with exactly those qualifications. There was only one problem. He and his wife were assigned to another country; in fact, their crates were already packed.

Windows for the Word

David and Sandi Allison had been assigned to Bangladesh when they received word that the Department of World Mission wanted them to begin the work of the Church of the Nazarene in Albania. If being flexible is a qualification for a missionary, David and Sandi certainly qualify. Within two months of hearing the news that they were not going to Bangladesh, they found themselves in Albania.

But God had given them preparation for this challenging new field. In the spring of 1989, David was enrolled in Nazarene Theological Seminary in Kansas City. He was a Canadian bachelor, had attended Canadian Nazarene College, and had received a degree in agriculture at MidAmerica Nazarene College (now University).

Sensing a call to missions, David served in South America as a Nazarene in Volunteer Service for one year, 1989-90, with the Compassionate Ministries arm of the church. He was an asset to our work and used his expertise in the field of agriculture to minister to the people there. While in South America, a Work and Witness team from Kansas City came, including a nurse by the name of Sandi Zachmire. Sandi had graduated from Olivet Nazarene University and also felt a call to missions. She had earned a master's degree in nursing and worked as an intensive care nurse for several years where high stress was the daily routine.

September 1990 found both David and Sandi in seminary, and in January of 1991 they were married. One year and one month later, they were commissioned by the Church of the Nazarene to be career missionaries. On April 30, 1993, Sandi, David, and their two sons, Christopher and Brandon, arrived in Albania.

Any new country is a source of culture shock to missionaries, but especially Albania. Those first months were extremely difficult. There were periods when they went weeks without running water and days without electricity. With temperatures in the 20s, they were also unable to buy fuel for the backup heater. This would be a hardship at any time, but with a baby under a year old it was definitely a struggle. Even when fuel could be bought, the cold was pervasive. The gaps around the framing of the windows allowed for an ample quantity of cold air so that curtains waved happily in the wind even with the windows closed. It was "normal" to be without water and electricity for at least four hours each day. Finding edible meat was difficult, and it was not unusual to have to go to eight different shops to find 10 or 12 items.

Because of the dependence of many people on foreign aid, it was difficult at first to know if people really wanted to be friends and were hungry for God, or if they wanted something else from the foreigners. Either way, it was important to meet needs. Hermann Gschwandtner had given wise advice, "For one year do not do anything except study language and get to know the culture of the people you are ministering to." Albanian, or Shqip (Shcheep), is one of the oldest and most difficult European languages to learn.

If you add to the above challenges the sense of oppression that many times can be tangibly felt in this country, you might have a tiny window through which to view what they experienced. The hardships were softened by the knowledge that God had placed them there and that these were a warm and needy people.

A highlight for the Allisons that first year was the privilege of representing the Church of the Nazarene when the first complete translation of the Bible in the Albanian language was presented to the government. The presentation took place in the building that was built to memorialize Enver Hoxha.

Three weeks after the Allisons arrived, reinforcements came in the form of a 14-person mission team from Point Loma Nazarene College (PLNC), led by Dana Walling. The Allisons' crate came about the same time, so the team was able to help them unpack. Dana writes their story.

"That first experience was incredible. We arrived in Tirana amid the usual chaos at the airport. Fortunately, Gesina Blaauw was there, and she whisked us through the airport security and past the begging children with their well-practiced pitiful looks. It was a shocking entry for us. Soon we were sipping lemonade underneath the grape arbor at Gesina's and were quickly oriented to the country and what we would be doing. Later that evening we were taken to the Peza Valley. Seven of us were sent out to homes to stay with families while the rest of us stayed at the home of Gesina's friend 'Mama.' We fell in love with the valley and its people. Even though the language barriers loomed large, love found a way to penetrate.

"I remember the first morning. I woke up early with jet lag and walked out onto the porch. It was almost sunrise. The roosters were crowing, the donkeys were braying, and a mist hung over the river. Already the songs of the workers in the fields made their way to the porch where I was sitting. The green hills and the wheat fields now turning to gold were interspersed with wild red poppies. It was breathtakingly beautiful.

"Working in a corner of the field was Mama, who had stayed up late getting us settled. Here was this dignified woman bent over in a threadbare dress with a scarf tied around her head, weeding her garden with a 10" stick that had been sharpened with an axe. I went to the duffle bags we had brought and found a shovel someone had donated.

"Quietly, I went out and began working next to Mama. She tried to dissuade me. She called me 'Professore.' It seemed that she felt working in the field was below my dignity. To me it was an honor to be next to this woman who survived life in Europe's most atheistic Communist regime. This strong woman of faith was not waiting for the right tools, but seizing the opportunities of freedom, she was going to work *her* land, even if all she had was a stick! I traded my shovel for Mama's stick. I still have it as a reminder of the truths I learned in 'Mama's garden.'

"We worked almost every day in Gesina's warehouse. A 'Feed the Hungry' mercy ship had arrived in the port of Durres with a load of wheat and other food supplies, part of which was given by German Nazarenes. A team of Australians was unloading the ship into army trucks that Gesina had commandeered in her own inimitable way. We unloaded the trucks into the warehouse. Within a few days, we were able to deliver the wheat to farmers in the

Peza Valley. We were thrilled the next morning as we drove off to work to see the sacks of wheat we had delivered on the backs of donkeys headed for the fields.

"The following week we painted the Children's Palace in downtown Tirana, where the International Church was meeting. It was there that we met Ervin, who was a leader in the youth group. He spoke English and quickly became a translator for us. Ervin's grandfather was one of the top government officials when the Communists took over the country. He was executed, and Ervin's family was blacklisted. Ervin was not able to enter the university until the regime fell, and by then he was 21 years old. One thing led to another, and some time after the visit from a group of education professors from PLNC, Ervin was able to go to PLNC, where he is currently a student. He has helped lead our two most recent teams to Albania and is a valuable asset to the college.

"Our team also painted the school in the village of Pajan. The people were so appreciative that they attended a service we held in the valley our last Sunday, even though they are traditionally Muslims."

Since that first trip, PLNC has contributed much to this country they have adopted and plan to have an ongoing ministry. A team of educators conducted workshops with the headmasters of schools from around the country. For three successive years in the spring, education professor Jim Johnson has led education teams that accompanied short-term mission teams. Ruth Grendell, professor of nursing, has also been in Albania consulting on health career issues.

— Nancy Hardison, a business professor from PLNC, has worked in Albania four different times. The last was a year's stay on Fulbright Scholarships with her husband, Gerry, a medical doctor. Nancy has been involved since the fall of 1992, when Hermann Gschwandtner asked her to give lectures in Albania on the topic "How to Start a Business." On March 30, 1993, she and Hermann were in Tirana ready to begin the lecture tour. They were barely off the plane when a missionary mentioned that the ministry of education was looking for help in training school administrators. Nancy suggested PLNC's graduate education department and faxed the director immediately, asking for help.

Nancy writes, "We arrived late to the first lecture several hours away, but the group was still waiting. There was no electricity in the entire city, so I gave the evening's lecture in the dark. It was a different experience for me, but the people were lively and wonderful. For three intense weeks I traveled with Adriana Bejko, my translator, and Gesina's car and driver. We ended every lecture by saying, 'The Institute for Total Encouragement represents people who are here because we love God and our neighbor.' When I left, I realized that I had to go back." Nancy has continued to work with David and Thoma on many business projects and loans to help farmers and other small businessmen recover economically.

In May, the same month the PLNC team arrived, Les Wooten, a Nazarene pastor from Illinois, came to Albania with Every Home for Christ (EHC). David and Sandi met with him and listened to his burden for the city of Lushnja, which had no church at that time. There had been an Every Home for Christ Crusade in that city some months before, and many people had written to the EHC office in Tirana, asking for a church in their city.

Rev. Wooten begged the Allisons to go and start a church for these people. Even though they had only been in language training for three months, David began to go every Saturday. Since they had no vehicle, it was a two-hour ride by bus. He visited the people who had written to EHC and eventually gathered some together for a Bible study. Sonila and Esmeralda were two of these first contacts. Later, Sandi Allison also went and led a children's ministry while David worked with the youth and adults. They found that the only ones really interested were children and youth. To one of these meetings came Gentian Hila from Gorre, a small village southwest of Lushnja. He begged David to come to his village to help him start a church. He assured him he would take a leadership role once the church was started. Gentian was 17.

The summer of 1993 was an eventful time. A young schoolteacher from England, Hilary Evans, came for four weeks, stayed with David and Sandi, and taught an intensive English course in the elementary school there. Something happened while Hilary was there those few weeks. She lost her heart to Albania, and like so many others she would return.

In October, the Allisons began going to Gorre every Saturday. From the beginning there was a group of 10 to 20 teenagers, mostly male, with one adult man. This group grew steadily.

In November 1993, the rigors of this new life proved too much for David and Sandi's unborn baby. It was the fifth month of pregnancy when she lost the baby and began hemorrhaging extensively. Denny Nolan, a plumber from Olathe, Kansas, and two of his friends were in Albania on an emergency trip to install plumbing and water storage for the Allisons. Though the men were staying in other homes, Denny "happened" to be there that night and was able to watch the children while David went to get the missionary doctor.

Since the conditions in the local hospitals were unsafe, the doctor tried to stop the bleeding but finally told David there was nothing more she could do. Their only hope was to get to a hospital in Thessaloniki, Greece. It was an 11-hour drive, and at 10 P.M. there was no possibility of buying gasoline.

Denny finished the story, "At that point Gesina Blaauw was contacted. She in turn contacted, by short wave, Swiss Helimission, a helicopter relief agency, about a medical evacuation. Around 3:30 A.M. two pilots came up the road, assessed the steep slope, and decided to take off from a landing zone outside of Tirana. David and I loaded the suitcases in their van and went back to make final arrangements with Gesina. While there, someone broke into the van with a pick-axe and took suitcases, supplies, money, and everything else! When I looked at David, he was devastated. His wife was dying, their vehicle had been vandalized, they had just been robbed, yet he managed great composure as we walked back into the house.

"We carried Sandi down the side of the hill to the van, with the two children crying and the doctor praying. It was probably one of the saddest sights I have ever seen. I turned to the doctor and asked how she felt about Sandi's condition. She said she was deteriorating quickly and only a miracle would save her. After the doctor left, I went back into the house, fell on my knees, and cried out to the Lord on Sandi and David's behalf. It seemed as if heaven came down around me. About 6 A.M., I walked to Gesina's and waited for the helicopter to come over us. High winds prevented an early take-off, but finally we heard the chopper and watched and prayed until it cleared the mountains and flew out of sight.

"The pilot was flying without radio contact and with only a city street map of Thessaloniki. He set the craft down within two blocks of a waiting ambulance, which rushed Sandi to the hospital where a surgical crew was waiting. The doctor said that only a miracle from God had saved her life."

God is so good! How awesome! The enemy meant it for evil, but God made the difference. His angels, in the form of Denny Nolan, Gesina Blaauw, and the Swiss Helimission, were on the spot to "bear her up" and carry her to safety and life. In January 1995, God gave David and Sandi a beautiful, healthy baby girl named Sarah Elizabeth.

In March of 1994, David Allison went to the airport to meet us, Bill and Connie Patrick, the first Nazarenes in Voluntary Service (NIVS) in Albania. We stayed with the Allisons for three weeks, and for two of those weeks the Allisons were able to go to Greece for a much needed rest while we guarded the house. It had only been four months since Sandi was evacuated to Thessaloniki, so they were all still recovering.

The atmosphere in the house was cold and damp and therefore inhospitable to these warmth-loving Californians. Looking back, I think it was the coldness inside the damp concrete walls that was the most difficult to endure and that made us wonder at times if we were going to be able to tough it out for our 12-month commitment. Usually, the instant cure was to put on our warmest clothes and take a walk down the street where we were welcomed in almost every shop and doorway. To hear their caring "Si jeni?" (How are you?) and "Yu mires?" (Are you well?) made our world right again.

Those first two weeks we survived the shock of riding in Albanian buses. Many cultures in the world do not have the same two-foot personal-space rule that we westerners have. In fact there is not even a two-*inch* rule if there are not enough buses at the right times.

We learned how to shop for vegetables in the open market and who we could trust to give us the correct change. We tried out our slowly accumulating language skills. Those dear people did not even snicker when I tried to tell them, "I am very busy," but instead was saying convincingly, "I am an egg, very much an egg." They were probably sadly agreeing and were amazed by the fact that I possessed such an honest assessment of my mental state.

When David and Sandi returned from Greece, refreshed, it was time to go to work. We had language lessons two hours a day, four days a week for six weeks, but that was only part of our daily schedule. With no telephone, every appointment had to be arranged in person, and international communications were often a nightmare. Getting into and around Tirana is, by itself, a stressful task. The streets were not made to handle the ever-increasing load of traffic.

Private citizens were not allowed to own a car during the Communist regime, therefore almost no one had driven for many years. So Bill helped by being general roustabout for David and Sandi while I relearned how to cook with what was available, became acquainted with my new neighbors, and taught beauty classes to the young women of the community. Who would have ever thought that God could use my 16 years in the cosmetic business to share Him with beautiful Albanian women. The six sessions were titled Inner and Outer Beauty, and with every practical lesson on cleansing, moisturizing, and caring for the skin, they were given a parallel spiritual application for their hearts.

Though there did not seem to be much understanding of the spiritual realm, many seeds were sown. Later, I would teach English classes from the Book of Mark. Students were confronted with the person of Jesus from the very first lesson. It was exciting and fulfilling work.

There Is a Church in the Window

The weekends proved to be our greatest challenge and one of the greatest rewards. We would get everything ready Friday night or early Saturday morning—food, clothing, bedding, and so on. By nine o'clock we were on our way, bouncing, jiggling, braking, and jerking for nearly two hours on the exhausting road to Lushnja. The tough ride was due not only to the very poor road surface but also to the unexpected animals, hay carts, bicycles, football-sized rocks in the road, and cars stopped with the drivers chatting to friends.

We would arrive in Lushnja with a great sigh of relief and slowly unbend as we exited the van. After Hilary came to Lushnja, she was always there to greet us cheerfully and serve a good cup of English tea. But in "the days before Hilary," we drove straight to the post office and began unloading the supplies for the children's service. There were between 30 and 50 children in the third-floor meeting room every Saturday. David began the service, Bill played guitar for the singing, and Sandi told the Bible story to the children in carefully written out Albanian.

As soon as this service was finished, we prepared to go to the next, this time in Gorre, 15 minutes by car down a country road. David would stop along the road to pick up any young people who were walking to the 4 P.M. service. There were always people waiting when we arrived. Initially, we met in the back room of a dingy store and were glad for the opportunity to rent it. Later, we were able to move across the street to what had been the dining hall of the former farming commune. The room was large with one large wall of windows, so it was much more cheery.

As you looked around, you noticed there was a core group who took responsibility for the service being set up—including chairs, songbooks, and the air of expectancy. These 8 to 10 high school students were beautiful in their spirit as well as their physical appearance. They seemed so bright, eager, and possessing of leadership qualities. Although they were young, suffering had brought a maturity beyond their years. Their hunger for the Word and thirst for righteousness seemed insatiable.

Before graduation they invited us to their end-of-the-year school festivities. It was our first time to be in an Albanian high school. The condition of the buildings and lack of equipment were depressing, but the excitement of the students over their presentation was the same as in Western schools. Bill had taught high school music for 20 years in California, so the electric atmosphere made us feel right at home.

The program began. There were skits and singing groups, more skits, poems, and songs. Fifteen minutes into the program we realized that 85 percent of everything that was happening was being done by "our young people." They were the school leaders, academically, artistically, and socially. When Gentian Hila became a Christian, these were the friends he had brought to the old store for David to preach to that first day. These were the people God chose to be the core group for the first Church of the Nazarene in Albania.

Summer was coming. Commitments to Christ had been made and were deepening. What was baptism? Could they do it? When? Where? The date was set, the place was found, and the details worked out. The believers from Gorre would join with the believers in Lushnja. It was going to be wonderful.

In May, we were pleased to have additional workers added to our mission team. Judith Ripley came for six months as a volunteer and Hilary Evans as a regional missionary from the United Kingdom. Born to an English mother and Canadian father, Hilary was 18 and on a trip around the world when God showed her she would be able to live in another culture. Her training and experience as a teacher, a year at Bible school, and a diploma in teaching English as a second language were invaluable assets. But God also rounded off her missionary preparation by giving her a summer in Swaziland and five years working in her local church with children and women's ministries.

I asked Hilary how she knew that God wanted her in Albania. She writes, "God first called me to be a missionary while I was in India. I knew from that point that I would live as part of another culture. Many years later in Watford, England, Hermann Gschwandtner came to talk about Albania. That very day I remember telling a friend I was going to leave Watford. I knew the time had come.

"When Hermann spoke to the church board, of which I was a member, he talked of the need for agriculturalists, teachers, and others. It was as if someone had put a hand on my shoulder and said, 'This is it. This is what you have been waiting for.' Amazingly, the rest of the church board looked at me and knew also. I asked Rev. Gschwandtner what I should do if I felt called to Albania. He said I should go for a month, and if I still felt called, then it certainly was of God, for I would not want to go of myself. With that advice, I prepared to go. It was May, and I left in September. That was enough time to notify the school where I was teaching. Amazing things followed. My school gave me a month's leave beginning the first day of the new school year. Very unusual!

"When I first arrived in Tirana, I was not shocked by the way things were, as I had lived in countries that were poorer. What shocked me was the rubble and lack of motivation to do anything about it. I did not know the history, which was the key to understanding the devastation.

"Near the end of the month I attended a service in Tirana where a Scottish man was preaching. It seemed as if he was talking only to me as he asked, 'What is keeping you from coming to Albania?' Very strange, I thought, since I was the only person in the room who was not 'in' Albania!

"He continued, 'Is it your family? Is it your friends? Is it the conditions here?'

"To each of these questions I answered, 'yes, yes!' I was so unsure if I could do it.

"Then he said, 'How dare you! How dare you not give up these small things for God. How dare you not leave home if God is calling you. How dare you not live here as Albanians do. They have no choice in the matter as you do. Jesus gave up everything for you, and you are concerned about these little things? How dare you!'

"With tears streaming down my face, I accepted God's call to come to Albania."

Hilary's church, Watford Woodside, paid her fare and pledged to support her for two years. The British Isles South District made her their district project for the 1996-97 church year. The Eurasia Region has acknowledged her call and supported her in practical ways. And in February 1997, the General Board of the Church of the Nazarene appointed her as a career missionary to Albania.

Life wasn't easy for Hilary and Judith the first few months, living as they were in two separate Albanian homes. They were thrown head first into the new culture, but God brought them through smiling and victorious. I believe their favorite verse in those days was "I can do all things through Christ who strengthens me" (Phil. 4:13).

Hilary began taking over the children's ministry in Lushnja, as Sandi Allison was expecting another baby and was very ill. Besides her own language study of Albanian, she also began teaching English. This brought opportunities to speak about faith, the meaning of life, and why we should believe in God. Judith, an agriculture specialist, worked with the farmers. When school started again in the autumn, Hilary became a consultant for English teachers throughout the area. Everywhere these young women went they walked or rode the dirty, stifling buses, unless there happened to be a missionary with a car to give them a lift, and this was a rare occurrence. Later, however, God gave Hilary a wonderful vehicle that is perfect for the Albanian roads.

What is her role now? She writes, "Besides continuing my previous responsibilities, Bible studies in Ngurres and helping to set up another preaching point in Krutje, I am now a preacher! It is not something I sought to do, but I am finding it a delight to clarify for myself what the Bible is saying and then bring it to life for others."

* * * * *

Summer arrived suddenly, hot and sultry, two days before the Point Loma team arrived in Lushnja. They "melted and dried out" many times in the hot wind those three weeks as they hand delivered hundreds of copies of *Jesus—The True Way to Life* to every house they could find. They taught Vacation Bible School to as many children as could be packed into the meeting room. They made friends for Jesus and the church, and they were there when we held the first Nazarene baptismal service in Albania.

The old ramshackle bus bound for the Adriatic Sea left Lushnja filled to overflowing with candidates for baptism and their families. We formed a parade as we followed with two vans full of missionaries and the Point Loma mission team of 16 strong young people. Anticipation was evident in everyone, from elderly missionaries to non-Christian families, as we bumped along the rough roads until we reached the beach. When we came to the spot David had chosen, everyone piled out and found a place in the sand to observe or take part in the service.

Twenty-three young people from the ages of 12 to 26 stood excitedly awaiting this special sacrament, the acted-out symbol of their faith in the death and resurrection of their Savior, Jesus Christ. No one could become a candidate for baptism until they had completed a series of studies for new Christians and received full permission from their families. Also they were required to hand in a written testimony to show their understanding of the step they were taking. Most of the parents looked mystified and did not pretend to understand or want baptism for themselves, but they were quite happy for their teenagers to believe.

Finally, everyone was ready. David called to those who desired, to come and pray together. We huddled together, old and new believers, while someone prayed in Shqip, and another in English. David, Bill, and the candidates made their way out into the water. The tide was out, so by the time they were in deep enough water to carry out immersion, we could barely see the expressions on their faces. One by one David and Bill baptized them until they came at last to Gentian.

Gentian was the young man who, Saturday after Saturday, would ride his bike the 12 miles to the children's meetings being held in Lushnja and beg David to come to his village and preach about Jesus. As soon as he was able, David went to Gorre to find that Gentian had 20 of his friends ready and waiting to hear the Good News.

Now it was V-day. Many of the 20 had just received baptism, and David and Gentian could not hold back the tears of rejoicing over what this day meant to both of them. As Gentian came up out of the water, he raised his hands in victory as they praised the Lord. Those of us on the shore, including even the curious sunbathers, realized that something very special was taking place. The glory that shone from the faces of the newly baptized was beautiful to behold. We sang, prayed again, and shared the joy of new life, the resurrection life, given through Jesus our Lord.

* * * * *

That summer we began an adult Bible study on Saturday afternoons in Lushnja. At first, two or three adults came, but finally Andon, on whose property we met, was the only adult attending consistently. The rest were teenagers. When Andon would ask his friends to come and learn about God, there were three replies. Almost without exception the people 25 to 45 would give one of two answers: "I believe, but I'm too busy, for I must work to provide for my family," or "I cannot believe." Those age 45 and older would say, "It is too late for me. Religion is for the young. It's too late for me."

There were a few exceptions. Thirty-eight-year-old Andon, a high school principal, was one of these. When the government stopped restricting foreign radio broadcasts, he heard a group in England advertising an English course based on the Bible. He quickly sent for it. David Allison met Andon one day while in Lushnja and found he was anxious to practice his English and was agreeable to have Bible studies held at his home. This precious family of four generations became our family as we met weekend after weekend on their property. None of the women came to study, but Andon grew in the knowledge of the Word, and we felt he made a lasting decision to serve Christ.

A medical team from Youth in Mission came last summer also. They taught seminars on health and birth control and worked in the children's hospital in Kombinat and in a village clinic up in the hills. In general, they were busy loving the people surrounding the pallat where they lived. They, the women included, also dug a septic tank by hand and built two toilets in an elementary school in the Peza Valley. This school never had sanitation facilities until this time.

One of the nurses, Tammy Hudson, was a newlywed pastor's wife from Canada. She had believed so strongly that God wanted her to come that she and her husband made the sacrifice to be apart those six long weeks. We all felt when Tammy left that she would return to Albania and the next time she would not be alone.

The Birth of a Church

When school began again in the fall, we were all busier than ever with a Saturday noon Bible study and an evening worship service in Gorre. Somewhere during all those Saturday services in Gorre, Bill and David noticed that one of the young men, Arjan, would gravitate to Bill's guitar, before and after every service. He would try to make something good come from those strings stretched over pieces of glued wood. One day, David remarked to Bill that maybe he could give Arjan guitar lessons. Bill jumped at the chance, and in three months Arjan was playing better than he.

The next year Arjan went into the army to fulfill his military duty, but he never wavered in his faith and shared with the other army recruits his songs about Jesus. Arjan helped no fewer than 10 young men to receive the Lord and begin following

Jesus. Now that he has finished his military service, he is again playing for the church services and has also preached a few times.

**Arjan in the army. Now a civilian
again continuing to serve the Lord.
Arjan has a local preacher's license.**

By this time Hilary and Judith had a place of their own, so it was possible for all of us to stay in Lushnja overnight and hold services on Sunday. David would return on Sunday morning for Sunday School and visitation in Gorre, then back to Lushnja for a morning worship service.

Bill went early to the post office and attempted to clean up some of the dirt, which had blown through the missing windows, along with the mud tracked in on the children's feet from the day before. This was not an easy task with only a scraggly broom and no dustpan. Guitar lessons at nine o'clock were for two of the young ladies who led worship. By ten o'clock, Bill was teaching a Sunday School lesson with a translator, and at eleven o'clock playing guitar for the worship service where David gave the message. After the service came lunch, and then it was time to load up and start the trip home.

By 3:30 or 4:00 P.M. we would arrive back in Kombinat, trembling a little, but thankful to have made the hazardous trip home in safety. After unpacking and resting a little, we were off to a home Bible study with Mariana's family. At four o'clock we were sure we could not manage it, but by six o'clock God always provided the strength.

In March, David began classes to instruct all those who were interested in studying the doctrine and faith of the Church of the Nazarene. Randy Beckam came from the European Nazarene Bible College (ENBC) to teach membership classes. David had a sign made with the name and church logo and placed it in the hall where we met. Our people were very proud of that sign. It showed them they were a part of something bigger than just Gorre and Lushnja—an organization that is spread around the globe and one that cares about them.

On May 15, 1995, the first Albanian Church of the Nazarene was officially organized with 21 members. Thoma and Gerti came from Tirana and Kombinat. Several came from Lushnja. The majority were the group from Gorre. Rev. Hermann Gschwandtner came from Germany to conduct the service and take in the charter members. The church was founded, and organized in one day. What a day of rejoicing!

The majority of the core group of the churches in Lushnja and Gorre.

We had asked to extend, by six weeks, our year's commitment in order to be there for the organization of the first Church of the Nazarene in Albania. We were so glad to be a part of this historic day, but now it was time to leave. We had promised our son and daughter-in-law to be home with them for the birth of their first child.

With torn emotions and painful good-byes, the only way it was bearable was to entrust them to Jesus and sing quietly, "God will take care of you." We also said, "Maybe we can come for a visit and see you again." Our next assignment was to teach music at ENBC on the Swiss-German border, so it did not seem an impossible dream. Our hope was in a marvelous faithful God to continue and complete the work He had begun in them.

And our hope was not in vain. Another NIVS couple with four children had already come. The Zupkes had both worked behind the iron curtain and met while working for a mission organization. They returned to the United States to raise a family but never lost the yearning to go back to Europe as missionaries. They would live in the Peza Valley, work on water projects, and come into Kombinat to help the Allisons when needed. The tiny Bible study held at the Allisons on Wednesday evenings was beginning to grow and have a more faithful attendance.

The next year our dream was realized. We were able to make a return visit, and by that time the Wednesday evening Bible study in Kombinat had become a Sunday morning service. A former restaurant on the main street had been purchased, and people sat around the tables having coffee and visiting Albanian style. The singing began at the appointed time, and later David brought the Word to listening ears. I could not keep back the tears of praise and thankfulness to God. I looked across to see our former landlady and her children listening intently. Dr. Shpresa was also there every Sunday with her two daughters. Mariana sat next to me that morning. God is so good!

The Windows of Heaven Are Open

It is difficult for a foreigner to judge whether an Albanian has truly committed his or her life to Christ because, due to this deeply ingrained culture of hospitality, they will say whatever they think you want them to say. This is the only hospitable way to treat any foreigner who is a guest in your country. The rule of hospitality is to lavish upon them the best you have—even if it is all you have—and say whatever will bring them pleasure. Therefore, the test of time and changed lives are the only ways to determine if a commitment has been truly sincere. In reality this is the only measuring gauge in any culture. I would like you to hear a few testimonies of some whose commitment can be measured by this gauge.

Jasher

I have always believed in God and that one should follow and remain in a religion, but the dictator of our time did not allow us to believe. One day the door opened and Albanians were free to believe. After awhile I thought, "What belief should I choose, Islam or Christianity?"

God spoke to me in a vision one night. "Read the Bible. Read the Bible." Through this my thinking was changed, and turning my eyes to Jesus Christ, the Spirit of God came to live in me.

I am taking part in the congregation of the people of the Nazarene. There is a difference in my life both in actions and spirit. Now I need to grow in faith. I thank God who has helped me so much in these times, forgiving my sins and cleansing my heart. The Lord Christ is the mightiest power. I want to be permanently in the presence of God.

* * * * *

Jasher was a policeman for many years. Policemen in Albania do not have a good reputation. His testimony is a source of amazement for many. Lule, his wife, was a believer first and prayed fervently that Jasher would be saved.

Lule

"Seek, and you will find. Your heart must not be afraid. Believe in God, believe also in Me" (see Matt. 7:7; John 14:1).

These are the precise words that brought me to the realization of faith. When I was saved, there were many things that were unknown to me. I did not know who created me, the reason for living, or that I was a sinner. I liked the way I was but thought only of myself. Something in me was missing. For me, the Lord existed in secrecy, and I did not know what to do about it. The thoughts about my life were clothed in obscure darkness.

But now, for four years, my heart has been wonderful. My first contact with Christianity was with the book *Jesus—the True Road to Life*. After studying it, I found Jesus as my Savior. I decided to follow His way (John 14:6). In the Church of the Nazarene we hear the words of God, worship the Lord, pray, and believe. This brings our spiritual growth. Thank God He has also given me different talents to work in His church. This is a gift I gladly receive.

Sonila

At first I heard about Jesus from the books that were spread around Lushnja by some Christian people. After some months, they invited me to go to the Nazarene meeting at the post office.

When I went, I found it was a children's club. Sandi was there, and she came to meet me. It was near Christmas. I didn't know anyone else there, so I stood alone at one corner of the hall watching the children as they prepared for the Christmas service. Even though I was alone that day, I was very happy. I did not know why at the time, but now I understand it. God wanted me and gave me that joy and happiness because it was His plan for me to stay there and learn about Him. Time passed, and I received Christ, was baptized, and have now been a Christian for three years.

That first day I was very happy to see those children in plays and dramas, but now I am very happy because I am able to lead that children's club. It is amazing! Our Lord is mighty, and He is an awesome God. I hope and pray to always be strong in faith and to worship and give praise only to my Lord Jesus Christ.

Roland

My father is a strong atheist and was modeled by communistic ideology. Therefore, I had problems in my family between me and my parents. My life was a loss (nothing). I was always worried and upset and often cried about my life.

In 1991, I registered and was admitted to an army college in Tirana. Communism was, at this time, being overthrown. The wall in Berlin fell. In college, I knew some friends of the Catholic tradition, and they invited me to go with them to church. I went to receive something. A cross in a bottle was being given, so to be the owner of a cross, I went. Instead, the priest gave me a cross and a Gospel of John. As I read, it was as if a burden was thrown off me. I began to find life.

In one year, the college was closed and I returned home. Chickenhearted, afraid of the present and the future, I began to pray a few words and knelt under the cross after the Orthodox tradition.

In 1993, my friend Gentian found a foreigner by the name of David Allison who talked about Jesus. I took an interest because God had already spoken to me through the Bible. I met with a group for 15 weeks to study a Bible course and received Jesus as Savior. My life continued to grow in faith. I began to understand more. I helped direct a young people's Bible study in Gorre. Our group took the initiative to share the gospel at school.

In 1995, I earned a place in the Skenderbeg Military Academy in Tirana. With the help of other Christians, I have begun a Bible study with my friends at the military academy. Through the years, the Lord has acted on the hearts of people in other countries to tell Albanians that Jesus is the Way, the Truth, and the Life. The Lord himself has expressed His love in John 3:16. God so loved Albanians that He gave His Son, His only Son, that we would not die but have His life eternal.

I greet you with the love of the Lord and God's blessing.

The Song Goes On

In *World Mission* magazine, November 1996, on page 6, is a picture of the restaurant that was formerly the Specialja. It was recently remodeled by a Work and Witness team from Kansas City First Church to be an attractive place to worship. Among the group pictured in front is Gerti, our most faithful teenager from the beginning of the Kombinat Bible studies. He plays guitar and leads music for the worship services. Dr. Shpresa is there. Lule and her husband, who became a believer just after we left, are standing with the neighbor they witnessed to and brought to church.

Gentian now has a local preacher's license.

Thoma is speaking in the services now and doing a wonderful job. Gentian, our leader from Gorre, who is now attending the University of Tirana, is providing strong support for the group and using his teaching skills in the Bible studies. Tuesday evenings they meet for prayer and Bible study, Fridays are set aside for a youth meeting, and evening English classes are always an attraction. Lord, You are faithful to keep what we have committed to You. Praise Your name.

Page 8 tells a story of Hilary Evans. There is a picture of her and a group of our teens from Lushnja, including Esmeralda and Sonila, two of our most faithful teens from the beginning. There is Landi, who feels God has called him to preach and is serious about following His call.

In the summer of 1996, Michael and Tammy Hudson and baby Julia arrived in Albania. They are our first designated church growth missionaries in the country, and we are excited they are there. At the moment they are stationed in Lushnja, which is a real boost both to Hilary and the churches in that area.

I asked Michael and Tammy to tell me how they knew they were to be missionaries to Albania. Michael tells the story.

"When we married in August 1993, Tammy was in nursing school in Hamilton, Ontario, and I was church planting in downtown Toronto. We were excited to be there serving the Lord together. In January of 1994, I was cleaning up the meeting room after a Sunday worship service and ran across a church bulletin from another Nazarene church in

Toronto. In it was a news clip stating that Youth in Mission (YIM) was sending its first medical team to Albania that summer. We knew the Allisons from seminary and had heard them on their deputation tour. My heart was touched by God to show the paper to Tammy before throwing it in the trash.

"We had talked before about the fact that I had the opportunity to go on four YIM summers and that Tammy would never be able to have that experience now that we were married and involved in church planting. Nevertheless, I sensed the Lord wanted me to at least show the article to her. When Tammy read it, she immediately felt that God wanted us to pray about it. There were huge difficulties to overcome. The application deadline was already passed, church planters and nursing students cannot afford such a thing, and it is highly unusual for newlyweds to be separated for six weeks. After praying, we both agreed that in spite of the obstacles we should call Nazarene Youth International headquarters in Kansas City.

"The team had already been formed, but the folks in Kansas City felt Tammy should be added. God laid it on the hearts of a couple in Tammy's home church to contribute a very large portion of her YIM expenses, and in June she was in Albania.

"When Tammy was introduced to the Allisons, they asked if she was related to T. M. Hudson. 'Yes,' she said, 'he's my husband. David and Sandi seemed a bit surprised, but we did not discover the reason until later.

"Four months before, a career missionary couple had been appointed to come to Albania. The Allisons had been wanting a permanent church growth couple for some time, but the needs on the Eurasia Region were rapidly expanding, so it was decided that this Albania-bound couple would be reassigned to another country. This still left a need for additional personnel in Albania. The regional director asked the Allisons if they knew of anyone who might be able to fit the need as they saw it. The Lord brought my name to their minds.

"This communication took place sometime in the spring of 1994, and in June Tammy showed up on their doorstep with the YIM team. David and Sandi did not even know I was married. This was the reason for their surprise.

"They did not tell Tammy any of this during the summer. However, they noticed that God was laying on her heart a strong burden for Albania. She was convinced by the end of her YIM experience that we were going to come back but did not know how. She was still in nursing school, we had not yet been through missionary candidate screening, and we could not afford to go as volunteers. But she was convinced this really was the Lord speaking to her.

"Tammy's presence and ministry in Albania that summer seemed to confirm in the minds of the Allisons that the possibility of our being appointed to Albania was of the Lord. They knew that because of Tammy's schooling, we would not be ready for appointment in 1995, but they were willing to wait.

"In October, I was asked to visit Albania to gain a better understanding of the work there. In the three weeks I was there, the Lord began to plant in my heart the same vision and burden He had given to Tammy more than a year before. Although it had been difficult for each of us to go to Albania alone, it has helped us to know that God called us individually to be here. Before the final decision, while praying separately, God gave to each of us the same scripture. It was an awesome experience!

"During our time of engagement and very early in our marriage, when we would speculate about the place God might be preparing us to serve, we said things like: pioneer area for the Church; a country with a Muslim influence; a place where we could plant a church, develop leadership, and provide compassionate ministry; a place maybe in the Mediterranean/Middle East area; and so on. These descriptions all fit Albania! We have no confidence in ourselves, but we do have confidence in our Lord and in His Church as together we yield ourselves to follow His Spirit."

There is not room to list all of the ways God has prepared these young missionaries for their assignment, but in courses of study, through experience, and through the molding of character, He has been faithful to prepare them well. For now, their job description is to learn the language and adapt to the culture. With the Allisons going on furlough in June 1997, they were to assume their responsibilities and continue to develop outreach, church growth, compassionate ministries, and the training of local ministers.

I asked the Hudsons to share one of the many things that helps them to survive when things are difficult. They respond, "Often, and in various ways, the Albanians have let us know they are glad we are here and they need us to be here. This makes us want to work even harder and do even more for the Kingdom and for their sakes—to join forces with them and be as committed to and excited about Jesus as they are. In many ways their Spirit-blown enthusiasm is the wind that fills our sails!"

And the work goes on, as do the challenges by the bucketful and the blessings by the ton. "Bless the LORD, O my soul; And all that is within me, bless [Your] holy name!" (Ps. 103:1).

Epilogue

In March 1997, the news report squealed over the BBC station on our shortwave radio, "Due to unrest over the failure of pyramid schemes in Albania, there is rioting in the capital, and many demonstrators have been burning government buildings in the South."

What was going on? What had happened? With 60 to 70 percent of the people out of work, living at poverty levels, and unschooled in the ways of money management in a market economy, many thousands jumped at the chance to make 50 to 100 percent interest on their investment. If they had no capital, they sold their homes, donkeys, whatever they could, to earn such great dividends.

At first, the organizers of the schemes delivered the promised amount, convincing everyone that investing was the only intelligent thing to do. Then, they left the country, taking the money with them. A vast majority of the Albanians were to lose at least half, if not all, of their invested money. The people felt they had been deceived again and directed their anger at the government for not protecting them. Many even believed that the government had profited from the schemes.

The anger escalated until armories were looted and everyone, including children, had access to all kinds of weapons. From March 1997 to the time of this writing in June 1997, the Albanians have lived in a state of anarchy because the military is not willing to fight their own people and the police do not have adequate firepower or manpower to establish authority. Children and adults are being critically wounded and killed, both by acts of aggression and random bullets.

The morning of March 12 the American Embassy advised its citizens to leave Albania. Before tickets could be purchased, however, the airport closed. The only alternative for our missionaries there was to load two vehicles with as much equipment as possible and drive to the port at Durres, hoping to take the ferry to Italy. All other escape routes were blocked by gunfire and looting. At the port, a flood of young Albanians attempted to storm the ferry, so the captain received orders to leave. Surrounded by growing anarchy, our two missionary couples with four children, three under the age of five, were left with seemingly no way out of the country.

March 12 at 5 P.M. was the last telephone contact our missionaries had with Southern Europe Field Director Rev. Duane Srader. At that point they called the Mission Aviation Fellowship logistics people in Tirana. They were told an evacuation was taking place at the port and it might be the last chance to get out. By now there were approximately 300 foreigners on the dock, about 150 of whom were missionaries huddled along a wall behind two vehicles. The wall was the only protection from the cold wind. Radio contact with the American Embassy indicated that the Italian Navy would evacuate them but would first take their own citizens. They were instructed to take only what they could carry easily and to lay facedown on the dock until they were cleared to board. At 11 P.M. the Italian and British military came with a landing craft.

By this time hundreds of armed Albanian men had assembled around them. As the Italians were boarding, the Albanians rushed the boats. The marines held them back with rounds of gunfire and then pulled out to sea leaving the missionaries again at the mercy of the anarchists. As the bullets and tracers flew over their heads, the group of missionaries were literally trampled by the Albanian men, some demanding their bags and purses at gunpoint.

David reports, "We were on the ground and could do nothing but try to cover the children as the Albanians climbed over us." As they worked their way across the prostrate bodies, little Julia was stepped on. The two mothers began kicking the assailants and yelling, "You are not going to hurt our babies!" The men amazingly stopped and moved away but not before Tammy's purse had been taken containing most of their means and antibiotics for their sick two-year-old.

Suddenly someone yelled, "They are looting in Tirana! We're missing out! That's not fair!" The men ran to find transportation to Tirana, some stealing the abandoned vehicles. Tammy wondered if it was an angel who had distracted the mob, for if they had stayed, everything would have been stolen. Twelve-year-old Christopher recounts, "The children were crying. Everyone was screaming. Then some were praying, and some began to sing. It was so cold and the concrete was so hard."

At daybreak the rescue mission returned. Miraculously, they were loaded onto the landing craft without incident, ending a more than 40-hour ordeal. They were taken by Italian carrier to Brindisi, Italy, not knowing if everything left behind would be gone when or if they returned.

David, in closing his report to the general church, pleaded for people to pray for the situation in Albania. "The believers are young and not yet tested. Pray for our lay leaders in all three churches, that our absence will spur them to recommit themselves to sharing the gospel."

At this writing, we see God abundantly answering our prayers. Eighteen-year-old Sonila writes, "We are all alone now. There are no missionaries to help us, but I think God is with us, and His Holy Spirit will help us. For three weeks the government forbade group meetings, but now we are conducting services and children's meetings on our own."

When David, Michael, and Duane Srader returned on a reconnaissance trip in May, they took in three new members in Lushnja. Vehicles and mission property were safe. The Allisons were due to furlough for a year in May. The Hudsons and Hilary Evans were, for a time, in the south of Italy working on their proficiency in the Albanian language, but now have been able to return.

One missionary who remained after the evacuation wrote to the others, "When you return, know that it is not the same Albania that you left, and it will be a long time before it is."

Until the glorious day of His returning, God is still working in Albania and has placed the Church of the Nazarene there to make a difference. The International Church is committed to establishing a living, growing body dedicated to God's message of heart holiness. He has given vision and plans to help lift burdens and to find solutions for the deep needs that envelop this country. These plans will be implemented by obedient people to whom God will ask, "Will you come to Albania and help?" If God wants you to fill a place in His harvest field, are you willing to say yes? We are to work, pray, give, and "become all things to all people, that . . . by all means . . . some [might be saved]" (1 Cor. 9:22, NRSV).

The first priority is for many people around the globe to build a hedge of prayer protection for the missionaries, workers, teams, and new converts, as they proclaim Jesus by life and word for those who hear, that they will receive it. Then pray for finances, property, materials, and a continued government policy of freedom for religious expression. _The battle in Albania will be won or lost by prayer or the lack of it._ Will we be obedient and faithful? We hear again Arjan's song, but the words are changed:

> Oh, you who are busy but accomplishing little,
> Come, the Lord is inviting you.
> Wake up sons and daughters.
> Oh, wake up all.

31 May 98